Charlie Brown!

Selected Cartoons from
GOOD GRIEF,
MORE PEANUTS!
VOL. 1

by Charles M. Schulz

A FAWCETT CREST BOOK

Fawcett Publications, Inc., Greenwich, Conn.

GOOD GRIEF, CHARLIE BROWN!

This book, prepared especially for Fawcett Publications, Inc.,
comprises the first half of GOOD GRIEF, MORE PEANUTS!,
and is reprinted by arrangement with Holt, Rinehart
and Winston, Inc.

Printed in the United States of America

Good Grief, Charlie Brown!

KRINKLE

AHEM
HE'S SO CUTE... SIGH
I'LL BET IF WE WERE TO GET MARRIED SOME DAY, SCHROEDER, WE'D BE VERY HAPPY...
WHILE YOU WERE PRACTICING THE PIANO, I'D BE IN THE KITCHEN MAKING YOUR BREAKFAST...

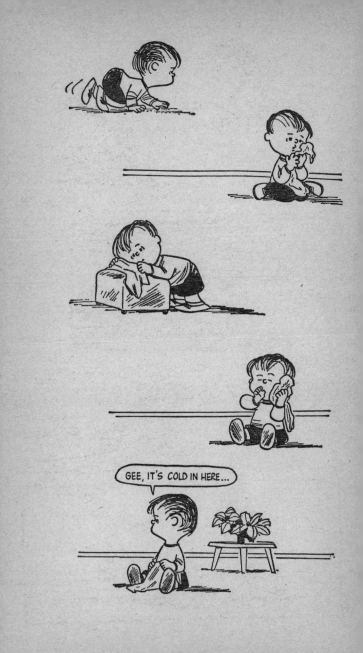